# Dry Stone Walls of Eryri

## Des Marshall

Gwasg Carreg Gwalch

First published in 2023
© text & photos: Des Marshall
Photos pg. 61-63 Ifan Lloyd Jones

All rights reserved. No part of this publication
may be reproduced, stored in a retrieval system,
or transmitted in any form or by any means,
electronic, electrostatic, magnetic tape, mechanical,
photocopying, recording, or otherwise, without prior
permission of the authors of the works herein.

ISBN: 978-1-84524-516-0
Cover design: Eleri Owen

Published by Gwasg Carreg Gwalch,
12 Iard yr Orsaf, Llanrwst, Wales LL26 0EH
tel: 01492 642031
email: books@carreg-gwalch.cymru
website: www.carreg-gwalch.cymru

*Dry Stone Walls of Eryri*

# Contents

| | |
|---|---|
| Introduction | 4 |
| History | 8 |
| Geology, Construction, Wall Features and Types | 14 |
| The Flora and Fauna of Dry Stone Walls | 52 |
| Stone Craftsmen of Eryri Today | 60 |
| Glossary of Commonly Used Terms | 64 |
| Useful Contacts | 66 |
| Further Reading | 67 |

# Introduction

'Wall' the dictionary says that this is 'a vertical structure made from stone, brick or wood with a length and height much greater than its thickness, used to divide, enclose or support'. I have always wondered why the land is so markedly split up into small parcels of land when I have been out walking, marvelling at the hours, days, months and years that were spent building these walls. I asked myself what use is that little strip of grass, what can it be used for? How and why did walls evolve? Where did 'wallers' get all their stone to build the thousands of miles of what appears to be randomly placed stones? Was it dug up or very unlikely just littering the ground? Was it all carted in from somewhere? Why are there different styles of wall? Those questions are, hopefully, answered in this book which is purely a guide to the stone walls of Snowdonia and is no way intended as an instruction manual.

Walls throughout the land have different styles and different rock types. Here in Eryri (*Snowdonia*) the rocks that form walls are generally igneous (volcanic) in origin, whilst in places such as the Peak District they are composed of sedimentary rocks such as millstone grit (gritstone) or limestone. Building such a wall is a slowly dying art. Walking around the valley floors or on the mountains there are many walls in a sad state of disrepair. Gaps in them have not been repaired and have been replaced by ugly post and wire.

There are many types of construction but the main criterion is the wall should have a wide base and a narrower top. Through rocks, known as through-stones, bind the wall together and helps to stop it falling down. To gain access from field to field gateways were made that allowed, initially, horse and cart to pass through, then latterly tractors and the like. Where mechanical access is not required stone step stiles were constructed. Through slabs of rock from one side of the wall to the other allowed people to cross. Sometimes narrow slit stiles allow access from one field to another. These are wide enough for a human leg but not larger creatures like sheep or cows. In some cases other walls, in conjunction with stone step stiles, have a gate to pass through at the wall top. No doubt farmers were thinking that their sheep are canny creatures and can suss out their escape from one field to another by climbing the steps. However, opening a gate is usually beyond their capability! Modern day wooden ladder stiles are often used to allow walkers to cross from one side of the wall to the other.

Low holes below walls allow animals such as sheep to pass through. Known as smoot, creep or hog holes, as well as localised names smaller creatures can pass freely. These are easily blocked if not needed by bits of corrugated sheet, old bed heads or even nowadays by a pallet. Sheep pens were built as, too, were sheep dip enclosures. These are clever in design and usually adorn remote valley floors. This book does not cover walls where cement is used to bind stones together. However, one type of wall called a *clawdd* (plural *cloddiau*) uses earth and grass to bind stones together. They are generally not very high. Being constructed of 'natural' material these are included.

It is important to remember when walking either in the mountains or along the valley floor NOT to climb over walls. If you find you have to climb one you are in the wrong place. Retrace your steps and find either a gate or stile on a recognised footpath. All too often this does not happen and walls become damaged. It is a very costly job repairing them if a dry stone waller has to be called in. If the farmer has to repair a wall himself it is a very time consuming job and an un-necessary waste of his time. Another far more waste of the farmer's time is when gates are left open and sheep can mix from one farm to another. It can take a couple of days of sorting sheep into their rightful parcel of land and could inevitably involve several farmers!

The best maps to use are the Ordnance Survey Outdoor Leisure 1:25,000 series. These give much greater detail by showing walls, fences and the patterns they create. Ones needed for this guide are: Outdoor Leisure 17 Snowdon/Yr Wyddfa: Outdoor Leisure 18 Harlech, Porthmadog & Bala/Y Bala and Outdoor Leisure 23 Cadair Idris & Llyn Tegid. I have not given a map reference for each wall or feature illustrated in the book but I have described its approximate location. Please also remember that some of these sites are in mountainous country so please dress accordingly. Take food, drinks and in summer sun screen. In winter pack a hot drink and extra clothing. Take any necessary medication needed for the day too! Also carry a compact first aid kit for small injuries. Know how to use a map and compass. They don't need a battery or rely on satellites that electronic devices such as GPS or smart phones need.

All the sites mentioned can be accessed by public footpaths, tracks or road. Be aware that parking on some roads is very restricted. PLEASE do not block gateways or track entrances. In essence abide by the Country Code and take ALL your litter home. The cans or bottles of drink you brought with you full, therefore heavier, when leaving home but when emptied are much lighter after being consumed. Please take these empties back home to dispose, as well as the remains of any uneaten fruit such as apple cores and fruit skins including banana and other fruit peelings. One last plea PLEASE keep your dog under control by having it on a lead especially when sheep are around. Many dogs see sheep as playthings but sadly a great number of them are terribly injured or killed by freely roaming dogs. Remember farmers have the right to shoot any dog seen molesting sheep!

**The Country Code**
Respect other people
Consider the local community and other people enjoying the outdoors
Park carefully so access to gateways and driveways are clear
Leave gates and property as you find them
Follow paths but give way to others where it's narrow
Protect the natural environment
Leave no trace of your visit, take ALL your litter home
Be careful with BBQs, avoid using single use ones and don't light fires
Keep dogs under effective control
Dog poo – bag it and bin it, or take it with you. DO NOT leave it by the side of the path or adorning a wayside tree to be picked up later as this rarely happens
Enjoy the outdoors
Plan ahead, check what facilities are open, be prepared
Follow advice and local signs and obey social distancing measures

NOTE: I have used traditional Imperial measurements for size and length rather than metric as these were the ones traditionally used. As a rough guide
    2.5 cms = 1 inch;
    30.5 cms = 1 foot.

# History

The art of dry stone walling is very old. How old, we do not know, but it was certainly one of man's earliest skills to be developed as shelters, fortifications, burial mounds ceremonial structures and animal enclosures were built. The Neolithic village of Skara Brae, built around 3,000 B.C., is a wonderful example of the skills these ancient people had. Also in Scotland the Iron Age 'brochs', fortified buildings, have withstood the test of time. Perhaps in the late Neolithic period mortar was discovered although in Egypt mortar was certainly being used in 4,700 B.C. This meant that stones could be 'cemented' together and not held in place purely by the weight of the stones as in a dry stone wall. That said, many of the dry stone constructions have outlived those using mortar! This is due mainly to wind and rain eroding the mortar and loosening stones that had been placed without much thought relying on the cement to 'glue' them together.

Dry stone walls have been constructed since, at least, the Stone and Iron Ages as stone is the most common type of construction material.

*Skara Brae, Orkneys – passages, huts, hearths, ancient and reconstructed (Images: WikiCommons)*

NOTE: The Stone Age began about 2.6 million years ago, the earliest evidence of humans using stone tools. This lasted until about 3,300 B.C. when the Bronze Age began. It is typically broken into three distinct periods: the Palaeolithic Period, Mesolithic Period and Neolithic Period.

*Dry Stone Walls of Eryri*   9

The Iron Age started between 1200 B.C. and 600 B.C. following the Stone and Bronze Ages. During the Iron Age, people across much of Europe, Asia and parts of Africa began making tools and weapons from iron and steel.

In the Stone Age, for example, people would not have tools available to them so great skill was needed to place stones so that each would interlock securely with others around them. People building these walls worked in gangs under task masters and under great scrutiny. Even today a good 'waller' will never pick up a stone and not place it in the wall. The stones laid are held in place by a combination of friction, gravity and the skill of the their placement by the 'waller'. Along with hedges, dry stone walls are the most common means of making field boundaries in the UK. It is possible there are no two fields of the same dimensions.

In the 'dark ages' dry stone walling fell out of favour. Settlements established by the Anglo-Saxons tended to be in lowland areas. However, in mediaeval times settlements were made at higher elevations. As such dry stone walling became much more prevalent. Stone was freely available in great quantity in these higher areas. The greatest amount of dry stone walls seen today date from the movement towards the enclosure of common farming and grazing land as society moved away from the feudal system. Building walls was also a good way of clearing the ground.

As more and more of the common land became enclosed so did the village people's rights to use the land rescinded. Mass sheep and cattle farming established itself. Small farms on the lower slopes of highland areas became enclosed by walls built of rough, irregular shaped stones. These date from the end of the mediaeval period to the late 16th century. During the 16th and 17th centuries dry stone walls started to appear at slightly higher elevations where sheep grazed. After the Parliamentary Acts of Enclosure of the 18th and 19th centuries walls were often built across very rough terrain making much larger enclosed areas or fields. By 1820 the walled landscape was virtually complete. Walls were kept in good order for a hundred years until the mechanisation of agriculture took place. Numbers of people working the land decreased and the demise of multi skilled farm labourers. By the 1960's walling as a full time occupation had almost vanished. Fortunately teams of conservation workers learned the skills from the few professional 'wallers' who remained.

Briefly, a word here about the Enclosure Acts. Around 1780 enclosures were promoted by the large landowners for their own benefit. These rich people had the means and influence to create private Acts of Parliament. This sadly stripped the small farmer of their rights. Each Act appointed commissioners who surveyed every plot and allotted portions to each claimant alongside proportional responsibility for enclosing the holdings. The set limit for walling these boundaries was only a year or two at the most and the lengths required were often many miles. As such 'wallers' were hired or men freed from their work on the land to build these walls. Sadly only the wealthiest people could pay for this cost. As such the other, poorer people had to forfeit their shares and land to the commissioners.

To sum up this process, it was a tragedy for the small man as he lost the right of pasturage on the common, lost his bit of land having to become a waged labourer in a time of falling wages and the rising cost of living. It secured the enslavement of the labouring classes. Land enclosure had begun in the 16th century by mutual agreement through the landowners. By the 18th century enclosures began being regulated by Parliament. A separate Act of Enclosure was then required by each village wishing to enclose its land. In 1801 there was a further rationalisation by a general Act of Parliament whereby any village could enclose its land where 75% of the landowners agreed. The common field had been subdivided into small more or less straight walled rectangular plots.

There were positive and negative impacts of these enclosures –

- Less land wastage as boundaries between the strips could be utilised.
- Land belonging to a good farmer was no longer impacted from the neglect of neighbouring strips.
- Machinery such as seed drills could be used on the larger plots.
- Farmers were encouraged to start crop rotation.
- Animal diseases became less likely to spread to all animals in the village.

- There were separate fields for animals which in turn encouraged selective breeding.
- Less labour was needed to look after the crops and animals as farms became more compact.

The negative effects affected many and included –

- The eviction of famers who failed to prove their legal entitlement to the land their families had worked for generations.
- Evictions of villagers who owned no land but had kept animals on common pastures. These common pastures were then allocated to other famers.
- Poor farmers who were only allocated small plots of land became unable to compete with larger landowners. As a result they lost their land when their businesses failed.
- Migration of the poor. After eviction they went to the industrial cities to find work. Unable to be self sufficient they had to accept poor wages and often dreadful conditions. Casual agricultural also suffered similarly.

In Wales the old Celtic field system slowly evolved into one of separate farms. These were surrounded by small fields with large areas remaining as 'common moorland'. Walling was the responsibility of the small farmer, even after becoming a tenant farmer to an absentee landlord. In 1894 a Royal Commission report stated that 'the stone walls in the neighbourhood were generally built by the tenant, except in the mountains, where sometimes the walls were long ones and these were built by the landlord'.

Observing walls today many wander somewhat raggedly, at times, up the mountainsides as well as traversing some pretty tricky terrain. Although ostensibly endeavouring to be straight they do weave around rocky outcrops and give a snake like appearance. Dry stone walls were inexpensive due to the plentiful supply of stone littering the mountains and cheap labour. Stone can also re-cycled.

So where did all this stone to build walls come from? Where none littered the hillsides rock was quarried from outcrops. No dry stone 'waller' would carry stones uphill if it could be avoided. Instead stones were rolled or, better, sent down on sledges. Two hundred years ago there were very few woodlands on the mountains due to the thinness of the soil. There was certainly no wire for post and wire fencing. Any materials other than stone would have to be carried uphill. Nowadays of course quad bikes and all terrain vehicles allow all materials to be driven up.

Looking at walls rather than just noticing them it will become apparent that there are often some pretty hefty 'boulders' placed in them. Another question begs itself here. How were these boulders placed? Two 'wallers' using a simple knowledge of leverage did this easily by using a two inch thick board some four or five feet long and were able to move rocks greater than the size of a tea chest or blanket box. Today the mind is energised to think about the men who built the walls seen straggling up mountainsides and to realise how skilled these people were. How, sometimes, the conditions they worked in were appalling ensuring that many remain standing to this day.

Sadly, though, today there is a distinct lack of skilled 'wallers'. Modern post and wire fencing is commonplace. It is cheaper with long stretches being built much more quickly. In my mind though these are ugly and characterless. It is a fact that a dry stone wall will last over two hundred years before a repair is needed whilst post and wire decays within a couple of decades littering the ground with rusty wire and rotten posts.

# Geology, Construction, Wall Features and Types

Throughout Snowdonia there is a vast array of rock types, igneous, sedimentary and metamorphic. Those of igneous origin have been formed by the cooling and solidification of magma or lava that had emanated from volcanoes. Sedimentary rocks include sandstone, millstone grit, limestone and shale. These have been deposited in lakes, by rivers or oceans. Much of the calcification of limestone for instance comes from countless billions of shells. Wherever limestone is found that rock was formed under the water surface. An extreme example where limestone is found is Mount Everest! Metamorphic rock occurs where the existing rock is altered to a different type. This occurs when the original rock is subjected to great pressures and heat. One of the best example of this type of rock is slate. Shale on the other hand is a fine grained *clastic* rock. This is a mixture of broken older rocks, clay and minerals especially quartz and calcite. It is unstable and splinters easily. Although very little is found in Snowdonia a classic example of shale is found in the Peak District at Mam Tor where the cliff facing the Hope Valley has slid and obliterated the main road.

Gwynedd and in particular Snowdonia has the majority of the oldest rocks in Wales and is geologically complex. This is reflected in the various types of wall that are seen in different areas of the National Park. The majority of dry stone walls are constructed from igneous (volcanic) type of stones along with slate. The Rhinogydd, however, is a large area of Cambrian grit sediments. These are very similar, but much coarser, than the millstone grit of the Peak District.

Igneous stones are coarse but very resilient to weathering. All manner of combinations can be seen, from rough igneous coping stones adorning rubble walls, slate coping stones on slate walls and slate coping stones on rubble walls. Elsewhere in the National Park igneous stones are also used for construction other than the slate quarrying and mining areas.

Here slate walls tend to proliferate. This happened when it became unsuitable for making into slates or other products and was, therefore, ideal for wall building. In the low lying Dyffryn Ardudwy area walls are much wider and constructed of more rounded stone. All walls are built on similar lines although to suit the local stone type. They were not uniformly unbroken as many have 'features'. For example, sheep creeps, drains allowing streams to flow beneath and stone step stiles amongst others.

In Snowdonia the stone used has a very random and awkward shape. Due to this the area provided the greatest challenge to the dry stone 'wallers'. The builders often referred to these 'awkward' stones as *pennau cwn*, translated into English as 'dog heads' due to their rough oval shape. Often these stones were dug out of the ground rather than quarried making them difficult to place. It was a skilled 'waller' that could make a secure, tightly knit aesthetic looking wall using these.

In some areas quartz coping stones were used to ward off evil spirits. The majority of walls were built during the enclosure period (1780 to 1820) and have much local history. In Cwmystradllyn, for instance, fields surrounding the Tyddyn Mawr tea room have numbers and names as shown in the diagram below. Cae is Welsh for field and Tyddyn Mawr translates as *big smallholding*.

790 – **CAE TAN BEUDY**, field before the cowshed, (literally under [below] the cowshed with tan being the corrupted version of dan)

791 – **CAE YR HOVEL**. Note the v. Nowadays f is pronounced as a v, so possibly now spelt with an f. Hofel is a hovel or cart house

794 – **CAE LLYN**, lake field

795 – **CAE CRWN**, crown field

797 – **WEIRGLODD FAWR**, big meadow (weirglodd is the shortened version of gweirglodd meaning meadow)

798 – **CAE LLORIAN**, breaking field (llori means to break perhaps referring to crumbling rock)

799 – **WEIRGLODD BACH**, little meadow

800 – **BUARTH**, yard

802 – **CAE BRWYNOG**, sad field

806 – **CAE PISTYLL**, water spout field. Pistyll is a spout of water. Often referred to describe a waterfall as in Pistyll Gwyn, (White Spout). Another term for a waterfall is Rhaeadr. This is a wider spread of water as in Rhaeadr Mawddach

807 – **CAE GEAR,** but possibly CAE CAER, field wall

808 – **CAE'R ODYN**, kiln field

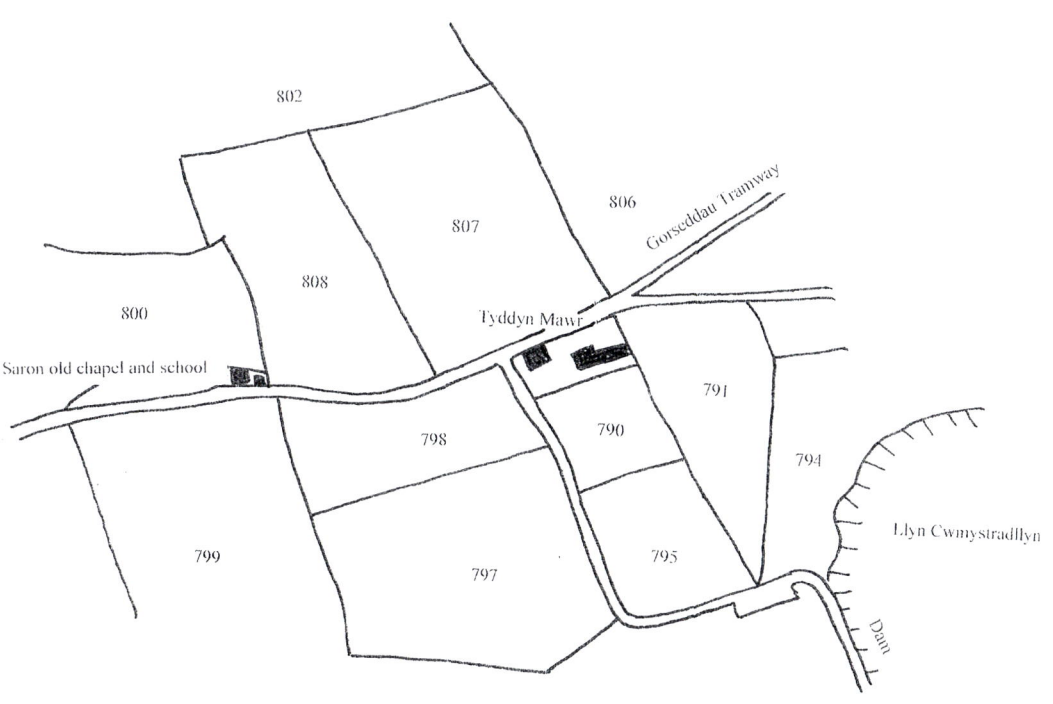

*Sketch of the wall pattern and field numbers surrounding Tyddyn Mawr, Cwmystradllyn*

Another type of wall, where stone is less abundant, are stone-faced earth banks. They became a traditional method of construction and called a *clawdd*, plural *cloddiau*. Not only did they help in clearing land that could be planted they also provided greater protection from the weather for animals and crops. These walls are lower but often have a hedge planted on top of them and perhaps, a ditch on one side. Traditional dry stone walls stand between 4 to 5 feet 3 inches high. Sadly the majority of walls and '*cloddiau*' are falling into disrepair at a faster rate than they are repaired. At one time they would have been repaired on an annual basis but changes in farming practises, especially labour and the ease with post and wire can be erected, walls are neglected. Repairs are costly but grants are available to ease the cost as walls will greatly outlive post and wire fences.

So what are the advantages of dry stone walls?

- They are durable when built properly with a great number having stood for well over 200 years and still look like they will go on for much longer. A post and wire fence lasts a fraction of this time.
- They are stock proof against most animals. Apparently black-faced sheep are renowned escape artists and need to be contained with walls at least 5 feet 3 inches high.
- They give shelter during all seasons. Shade when it is hot and on the lea side away from the wind and driving rain.
- They are easy to maintain.
- They drain naturally.
- They occupy only 28 to 34 inches at ground level.
- Stone is usually close at hand with no need to bring it in from elsewhere.
- Very few tools are needed. Those that are include a 4lb hammer, an 'A' frame, two strong pieces of string (nylon line), pegs for attaching the line, pickaxe, shovel, crowbar, sledge hammer and a tape measure.
- Finally, they cannot be burnt down.

If there are advantages what are the disadvantages? There are only a few.

- They take time to build and takes around a day to construct a 20 foot length of wall by 55 inches high.
- People are tempted to climb over walls. This activity dislodges stones especially the copings. A ladder stile is often used

where the wall crosses a path. Sometimes gaps have been created to allow gates to be utilised allowing the movement of stock from one field to another. Sadly gates are far too often left open by walkers. To avoid this the farmer padlocks them to avoid sheep intermingling with other sheep from a different farm. Sorting this problem out creates much un-needed work to separate them. Stone steps can be incorporated into the wall to facilitate the crossing, sometimes with a gate or hurdle on top.
- When walls are built close to a tree they can be weakened as the trees grow. During strong winds trees sway and their roots weaken the wall structure.
- The top stones are easily dislodged by animals such as horses. As such, the remedy is to place a length of barbed wire along the length of affected wall.

There is no definitive style for dry stone walling. It all depends on the stone available for each area. Most walls are built to a height of around 55 inches although this can vary. The base of a wall should be twice the width of it before the coping stones are placed. There are six ways stones are used in the construction.

- **Foundation stone.** These are the large heavy stones seen at the base. They are often irregularly shaped but capable of bearing the weight of the wall. It is very important that concrete is not used as a foundation for dry stone walls.
- **Building stones.** These are the stones used for the two outer faces of the wall. They are of varying thickness but the larger ones need to be placed lower in the wall to maintain stability.
- **Throughstones.** These are the stones that pass from one side of the wall to the other to tie the wall together.
- **Cap stones coping stones or copestones.** These sit on top of the wall and can be of various designs. Whatever that is they need to be tightly packed so that their weight bears downwards and ties the wall together. Shapes vary from area to area but the main criterion being they should be wide enough to span the top of the wall and be some 8 – 12 inches high. An interesting note here is that, occasionally, walls are seen with quartz being used for the coping. This apparently wards off evil spirits!

*Dry Stone Walls of Eryri*

- **Pins or pinnings.** These are small tapering pieces of stone used to lock either stones in the wall or the line of coping stones
- **Hearting.** These are the very small pieces of stone that are carefully placed to pack out the middle of the wall between the two faces as well as supporting the inner length of the wall.

The normal specification for a ***double dry stone wall*** is for it to be 4 feet 6 inches high. At foundation level the width should be 28 to 34 inches, whilst at the top it is 14. The slope of the wall is called the **batter**. **Throughstones** are set at 21 inches above ground level then placed at 3 foot centres along the wall to tie it together. Each one should project slightly on both sides. The **coverband** should project 2 inches on both sides. Walls are ideally built starting from the wallhead or cheekend.

In the mountains wall construction is what can be termed a ***single or boulder type dry stone wall***. These are constructed by placing stones the whole width of the wall and are most common in mountainous areas in all the northern areas of the UK. Obviously this includes Snowdonia and the Lake District where granitic rocks proliferate. These walls have large and often rough boulders which are placed in a single row wedged into position. Not only is this type of stone extremely hard they are extremely durable and rarely erode into smaller pieces.

Familiarity with the stone is most important in the construction of this type of wall often built by two 'wallers'. A good eye for picking the correct stone is necessary as each stone can be very heavy. Straight edges are virtually impossible to achieve. The largest stones are used for the foundation and dug into the ground and the wallhead needs to be well secured. It is important to ensure that any points on the stones being used do not point upwards as this makes securing subsequent ones more difficult and does not allow the wall to settle or for stones to tighten.

Having firmly set the foundation stones work can then commence on subsequent courses. If the stones are very large a plank can be set up as a ramp so that they can be rolled up and jammed firmly into place. If necessary any gaps can be filled by using pins to wedge stones securely in position. As the wall becomes higher smaller stones are used with stones set into position so that they lock into the gaps below. It is important that joints should be covered whilst at the same time ensuring a good bearing for the next stone. When the wall reaches the height required a line can be used to allow a level top to be made. A properly built 4 feet 6 inches high dry stone wall is impervious to wind at 3 feet above ground level with shelter on one side or the other. Fresh grazing grass is often found in a field on the sheltered side of a wall.

When building on slopes construction becomes much more complex. On very shallow slopes stones can be placed that follow the slope of the ground particularly if the stones are flatter. Once the slope is greater than twenty degrees the courses are laid horizontally. Walls are built up slope. Foundation stones are placed in horizontal shallow trenches dug into the slope. Each trench is stepped up on top of each other. The steeper the slope the shorter each trench will be. On each step half a stone overlaps the one below.

On walls that climb steeply there has been much debate as to how the coping stones should be placed. Some say that these should lean uphill, others say downhill whilst a third thought says they should laid vertically! Also 'wallers' are equally divided whether coping stones should be placed from bottom up or from the top down!

*Steep slope wall construction above the Prenteg road, Cwmystradllyn. Note how the courses are level*

*Dry Stone Walls of Eryri*

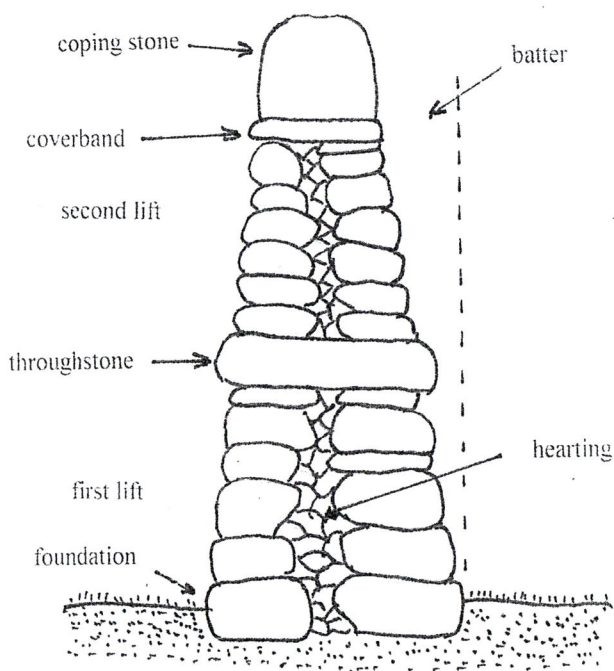

*Cross section of a double wall*

In lower areas double walls are constructed and much more commonly seen. These have what are termed two faces with their ends almost meeting in the centre of the wall. The small gap between them is filled with heartings.

The foundations for this type of wall are started by digging a shallow trench a few inches wider than the base will be by removing the topsoil, roots and vegetation. Stones are then laid on solid ground. These need to be large with their good face outwards, their flattest surface uppermost, reach into the centre of the wall and laid with their faces touching. When building double walls the foundation stones are placed on each side of the wall with their roughest sides towards the ground. Endeavouring to make as flat a surface as possible by using pins or wedges to level the surfaces up. Heartings are placed in the small gap between the two stones. Once the foundations are solid and as level as possible building can commence.

The wall is built methodically with the larger stones being placed lower in the wall. These bear the weight of stones above

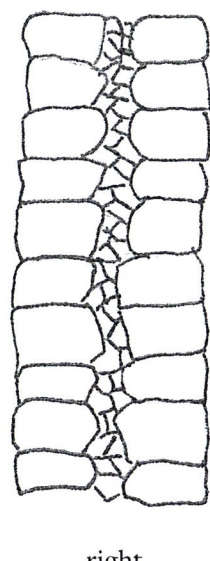    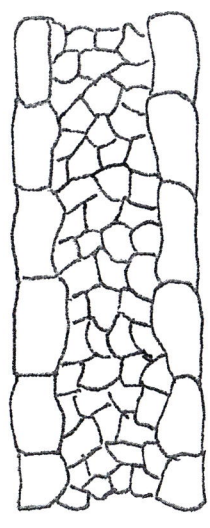

right    wrong

*The correct method of placing hearting*

them as well as reaching further into the wall. Each stone is placed and wedged firmly before another is placed. A good 'waller' never uses a hammer to bash the stones into place. Heartings are placed as each course is built. Each side of the wall is built at the same rate and kept at the same height as well as trying to keep the courses as level as possible. It is important that vertical joints are covered. Bricklayers have a saying of 'two on one and one on two' is most apt.

Once the wall reaches around 21 inches high, or thereabouts, it is levelled off and throughstones placed. These bind the wall together and placed no more than three feet apart. They do not want to project from the wall as animals can scratch themselves or bump into them that could make the top part of the wall unstable. They also need to cover the joints below them and be well supported under their centres.

1. A fine line of sloping coping stones on a wall above Cae-yr-eithin-tew, Cwmystradllyn;
2. New dry stone wall with coping stones near the Cregennen Lakes;
3. Decorative coping stones highlighted at sunrise close to the summit of Garnedd Goch on the Nantlle Ridge;
4. Slate dry stone wall at Oakeley slate quarry with bizarre copings above Blaenau Ffestiniog

The wall above the throughstones is known as the second lift with smaller stones being used for the remaining part of the construction. Once the height of the wall being built is reached coverbands are placed across the wall which is now around 14 inches wide or half the width at foundation level. Coping stones can then be placed so that their tops are level.

1. Close up of coping stones;
2. Rough coping stones on a wall with a stone step stile in a wall below Moelfre in the Rhinogydd;
3. Coping stones and solid wall foundations in a wall below Moelfre in the Rhinogydd. Rhinog Fawr in the background;
4. A new dry stone wall in Nanmor with unusual vertical slate slab and wire fencing on top

*Dry Stone Walls of Eryri*

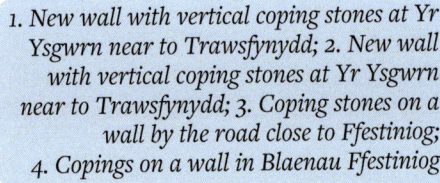

*1. New wall with vertical coping stones at Yr Ysgwrn near to Trawsfynydd; 2. New wall with vertical coping stones at Yr Ysgwrn near to Trawsfynydd; 3. Coping stones on a wall by the road close to Ffestiniog; 4. Copings on a wall in Blaenau Ffestiniog*

Wallheads or cheekends are perhaps the most common feature of a dry stone wall. They are built where walls stop, for instance where a gate needs to be fitted across a gap, or just providing gaps for animal access. If a large pillar of stone is going to be used as a gatepost a deep hole needs to dug and securely fixed before the wall is built. Usually this is now done using concrete! Normally, though, the wallhead is built first by using long stones in the same manner of coursing ensuring that a vertical joint does not develop.

1. Tall block used as a wallhead and gatepost;
2. Gate posts at entrance to Braich y Big farm in Cwmystradllyn; 3. Initials of a previous owner on one of the gate posts leading into Braich y Big farm; 4 Wallhead by the side of the Prenteg road from Cwmystradllyn;
5. Ragged walhead with an old iron gate hook above Cae-yr-eithin-tew in Cwmystradllyn

*Dry Stone Walls of Eryri*

1. Large upright stone used as a wallhead and gatepost above Cae-yr-eithin-tew, Cwmystradllyn;
2. Wall-end corner stone for two walls at 90 degrees to each other at Tyddyn Mawr;
3. Burial Chamber used as a wallhead below Moelfre, Rhinogydd;
4. A gap in a wall showing throughstones at a wallhead in Nanmor;
5. Substantial gateposts and modern gate at a field entrance in Cwmystradllyn

*Dry Stone Walls of Eryri*

Wall corners are much more complex to build. A tying in technique is used here in a similar fashion to the wallhead. The inner corner interlocks in a similar way to the outer one.

Stone step stiles are a fairly common sight in Snowdonia. Although there are two basic types the one most often seen is the stepped version whilst the other is a step through one. Here the gap is wide at the top but narrow at the bottom, They give access over walls and can be built in as the wall is constructed. There is, therefore, no need for a wood ladder stile. Occasionally there is a gate at the top of the wall to further stop livestock from clambering over. Sheep could possibly work out how to climb the steps but not fathom out how to open a gate! The step stile utilises three or, perhaps, four long, thick slabs of stone that project equally on both sides of the wall, wide enough for people's feet as well as being able to bear their weight. The first one is placed about a foot off the ground. The next steps are placed so that they overlap the rear edges of each of the stones below. This is done to stop people falling between any gap if they slip. The last step should not be placed close to the top of the wall as it needs the weight of stones above it to avoid it rocking and dislodging the coping stones.

The other type of stone stiles are often known as squeeze stiles and are occasionally found in the lower farmland areas where cattle are in fields. If sheep are present in these fields they could make an escape into the adjoining field if they think that the grass is greener! One type of construction starts at throughstone level and the gap constructed above it. Narrow at the bottom it becomes wider with height. The wallhead stones need to be larger than the main wall as well as the coping stones. Walkers tend to use the coping stones as support and are often pulled on when passing through. With this type of construction a lamb thinks the wall is an impassable barrier to get through but when it is has grown it will be far too fat to get through when trying to pass through! Another method of construction is to place an upright flagstone across the lower part of the gap making the walker step over it. This is embedded into the wallhead.

Another form of squeeze stile is where tall thick slabs of stone are erected at the wallhead. Their ends are dug into the ground and with a very narrow gap at ground level they taper outwards into the wall. The usual way of climbing over walls is by erecting a wood ladder stile over them although gates are now becoming more common.

1. Stone step stile and hurdle on a wall above Cae-yr-eithin-tew, Cwmystradllyn;
2. An old form of ladder stile close to Cefn Ddu slate quarry above Waunfawr. It has slate sides and iron rods used as steps

1. Ladder stile over a wall at the Cregennen Lakes;
2. Stone step stile and old bed head for a gate above Cwm Nantcol;
3. Stone step stile with gate on top near Dyffryn Ardudwy;
4. Stone step stile with gate on top of wall above Dyffryn Ardudwy

***Lunky, Hogg, Sheep Creep* or *Cripple holes*** are generally used in the more mountainous areas enabling sheep to have access into other fields owned by the farmer without the need for gates. Sometimes there is a stone step stile close that gives shepherds access over the wall. Smaller holes are sometimes used allowing lambs to pass easily to feed on untainted grass in the next field which could otherwise have been polluted by worm eggs dropped by the ewe.

Smaller holes such ***smoot holes*** were constructed into the older walls of Snowdonia allowing for the easy passage of rabbits and hares. In older days these were a source of food. These holes would often have netting fixed to them to catch these creatures. Where small streams are spanned by a wall ***watersmoots*** (*otherwise waterpens or watergates*) were constructed.

*Dry Stone Walls of Eryri*

1. Watersmoot in the wood to the east of the A470 level with the end of Llyn Trawsfynydd; 2. Sheep creep close to the Prenteg road in Cwmystradllyn; 3. Sluice opening in a wall at Tyddyn Mawr, Cwmystradllyn; 4. Slate carved feeding trough in a wall at Tyddyn Mawr, Cwmystradllyn; 5. Sheep Creep in the Rhinogydd with Moelfre in the distance; 6. Sheep creep in wall below Moelfre in the Rhinogydd; 7. A pair of watersmoots at Aberllefenni; 8. Sheep creep in a wall near Bronaber; 9. A blocked off sheep creep below Manod Mawr in Cwm Teigl

*Dry Stone Walls of Eryri*

Sometimes it is necessary to build a curve, especially when circumventing a tree or building a sheep pen. Good judgement is required and the iron bars and pegs are found to be very useful. To create the initial curve at ground level pegs are used in order to get as smooth a curve as possible.

Arches too require great skill. Ideal stones need careful sorting and preparing. Usually a template is made before construction commences. Each stone needs to have a regular shape as well as having a slight taper and span the width of the wall. As stones are placed it may be necessary to wedge them in position at the correct angle. Construction continues, building each side simultaneously. The final stone to be placed is the keystone. Ideally this should be wedge shaped. Once secured the wall above the arch can continue being built.

36  *Dry Stone Walls of Eryri*

1. Archway at Golwern slate quarry above Friog, close to Fairbourne; 2. Incline wall at Rhiwfachno slate quarry with archway for the tramway, Cwm Penmachno; 3. A dry stone arch at the Prince of Wales slate mill in Cwm Pennant; 4. The fine dry stone walled arch below an internal tramway at Bryn Hafod y Wern slate quarry near Bethesda; 5. A slate arch at Rhosydd slate mine above Cwmorthin; 6. A fine dry stone arch below a dressing floor at Hafod y Porth copper mine below Yr Aran above Craflwyn

Dry Stone Walls of Eryri

Embankment walls are often built to form a wide terrace to accommodate railway lines. These usually do not have coping stones. However, retaining walls in slate quarries were built to hold back waste. At Gorseddau slate quarry in Cwmystradllyn there is a remarkable curved overhanging retaining wall. This also protected the tramway from any waste deciding to cascade on to it. It is a wonderful feature and well worth the easy walk to see it. Retaining walls generally have a batter of 1 in 6 rather than the more usual one for dry stone walls of 1 in 8. They can be either double or single skin. One of the tallest of these is to be found on the Ffestiniog Railway. Known as Cei Mawr it stands proud at 62 feet high, reputedly the highest dry stone wall in Europe! Two parallel walls were built with the space between them filled with earth and rubble. At the top the width is eight feet and carries the railway track bed.

*Retaining wall construction. Shown with optional coping stones*

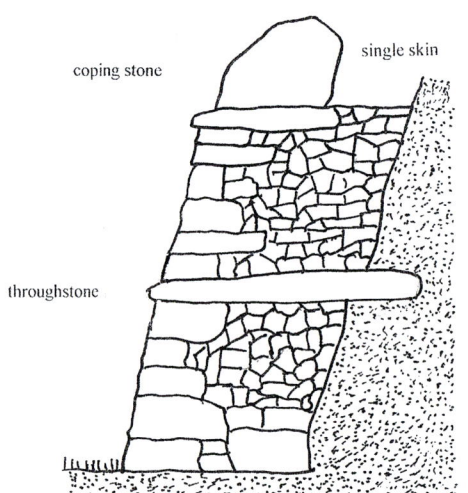

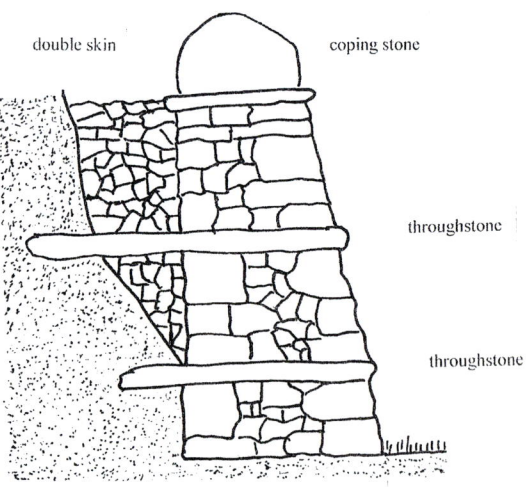

Many retaining walls are built across a slope to hold back debris, such as soil, stone or even spoil from a quarry, from sliding forward. Some even have coping stones. Building these starts, just like any other dry stone wall, from a firm foundation. Small holes are left between stones in the wall to allow for drainage at 2 to 3 feet intervals. Usually these are placed above the longer and flatter than usual

*The Ffestiniog Railway crossing a fine dry stone embankment in Coed Cae Fali*

throughstones. Before construction commences the banking being 'retained' is cut back to half the height of the finished wall preferably sloping the ground behind the wall away from it. As with other types of dry stone wall the foundations need to be firm and level. The length of the building stone runs into the wall just as it would in a double dry stone wall and not along the face of it.

*The overhanging protecting wall for the Gorseddau Tramway, Cwmystradllyn*

1. The Ffestiniog Railway crossing Cei Mawr embankment in Coed Cae Fali, reputedly the highest dry stone wall in Europe;
2. A retaining wall in Dinorwig slate quarry with an access arch at its base

1. A huge retaining wall at Rhosydd slate mine;
2. A tall very randomly built retaining wall at Cwt y Bugail slate mine above Cwm Penmachno;
3. Quarry retaining wall at Bryn Hafod y Wern slate quarry;
4. The decaying slate quarry retaining wall of Gallt y Fedw close to Nantlle;
5. The fine dry stone walled incline at Gorseddau slate quarry;
6. Dry stone built embankment for the Blaenau Ffestiniog to Bala railway line that closed in 1962;
7. An incline wall at Croesor slate mine

Dry stone walling is also used in the construction of sheep pens. Other names for these are folding, sheepfold or sheepcote. These are a feature in lower lying areas below mountains. Sheep brought down from mountain pastures are gathered in pens where they are sorted and processed. Folds were often constructed close to a stream where there was a stretch of deep water, although sometimes a dam had to be constructed to form a pool. The main feature of these pools was an opening from the enclosure. These were usually a simple oval shape or rectangular. Washing the sheep a few days before shearing cleaned and softened the fleece. Sometimes sheepfolds are seen at the intake wall, the highest wall seen on a mountain that crosses the slope of it.

Mountain enclosure dates from the late 18th or early 19th centuries which created many hundreds of miles of dry stone walls. This resulted in many rectangular folds of many different sizes being built whilst on the higher ground smaller folds were built into the corner of fields. Many of these are decayed and unused nowadays.

*1. Sheepfold in Pant Engan, Cwmystradllyn; 2. Sheep enclosure in a field above Traian, Cwmystradllyn; 3. Sheepfold by a wash pool in Cwmystradllyn below Gorseddau slate quarry*

Other dry stone built wall features include dam walls. These were built to create reservoirs for the slate industry and usually consisted of two walls separated by a gap which was filled with clay and rubble to make the dam more watertight. This type of construction also allowed for it to be built higher if necessary.

*1. The dry stone dam below the Prince of Wales slate quarry in Cwm Pennant;*
*2. The breached dry stone walled dam that held water back for Rhiwbach slate mine above Cwm Penmachno*

*Dry Stone Walls of Eryri*

Although I have not included dry stone built buildings there are many, especially associated with the slate mines and quarries. A selection of these are pictured here.

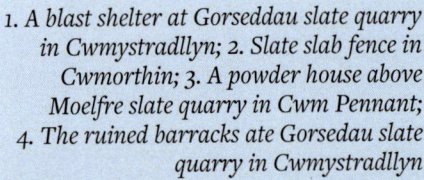
*1. A blast shelter at Gorseddau slate quarry in Cwmystradllyn; 2. Slate slab fence in Cwmorthin; 3. A powder house above Moelfre slate quarry in Cwm Pennant; 4. The ruined barracks ate Gorsedau slate quarry in Cwmystradllyn*

> 1. *Part of a slate post and rail wall at Rhiwbach slate quarry, above Penmachno;*
> 2. *Derelict buildings at Rhiwbach slate quarry of the old settlement;*
> 3. *The ruins of Cwmorthin terrace in Cwmorthin;*
> 4. *Pyramid used as an anchor for a 'Blondin'*

The tradition of dry stone walls endures and continues to serve the purposes they did hundreds of years ago when they first started to be built. The walls provide sanctuary for wild life in providing shelter in times of rain or wind as well as providing

creatures with a home. They also allow plants to flourish, as well as having their own micro climate. Dry stone walls are an enduring feature of Snowdonia and provide a most durable boundary between one field and the next outlasting any post and wire fencing.

*1. Dry stone walling on a pyramid at Dorothea slate quarry, Talysarn, Dyffryn Nantlle; 2. A fine wall corner on a building above Gallt y Fedw slate quarry in Dyffryn Nantlle; 3. Dry stone built wheelpit at Rhosydd slate mine*

Dry Stone Walls of Eryri 49

On a note of history it has long been a legend that the highest wall in Wales was built by French prisoners of war from Napoleon's army some two hundred years ago on the slopes of Foel Fras. This mountain is situated at over three thousand feet above sea level. This legend does have a foundation of truth in that French prisoners of war were held in Wales but it is unclear if any of them built this wall as it would have taken work away from the local people.

It is difficult not to wonder at walls snaking their way up huge mountainsides about the men who built them and how skilled they must have been. They worked extremely hard often in terrible harsh conditions, placing the wet, rough, slimy and awkward stones securely in position. I wonder if any of them received any recognition for all of this?

1. One of the streets and row of houses at the abandoned village of Treforys close to Gorseddau slate quarry, Cwmystradllyn;
2. Slate slab fence in Cwm Hengae, Aberllefenni

*Dry Stone Walls of Eryri*

# The Flora and Fauna of Dry Stone Walls

Traditional dry stone walls provide a whole range of habitats for wildlife as well as a huge variety of plants. Many of these are dependent on walls not only to germinate and thrive but to survive. Animals find walls a safe haven, not only as a sanctuary, but also, as a guide to navigation. One can say that in reality walls are a linear eco system and nature reserve in their own right.

They even have their own micro climate. One side is exposed to wet weather whilst the other is protected and is drier and warmer. The top where the coping stones sit is windswept. However, the wall bottom is sheltered inside of which it can often be dry and cosy for small creatures. Every wall is different. Each will be a collection of micro-habitats. Walls high up on mountains are much more random in their construction and differ greatly from those at lower levels. Here walls are home to literally many genera of plants whilst dozens of creatures make them their home.

The more well constructed dry stone walls are not without their 'inhabitants'. These hide in the tiniest of nooks and crannies. Creatures such as spiders, woodlice, springtails, millipedes, bees and wasps often make walls their home. Toads and slow worms share the environment at the bottom of the wall with field mice, shrews and hedgehogs. Birds such as wheatears often lay their pale blue eggs within if a cavity is at low level. Robins or redstarts are often seen in walls bounding woodland whilst in open farmland little owls can be found in the larger cavities deep inside. In the absence of trees coping stones provide perches and view points for birds of prey to pounce. Bats are also known to inhabit walls. These prefer a letter box type opening with the narrow slit immediately below the coping stones of the higher walls.

In long stretches of wall gate or gap free walls 'smoot holes' are constructed. This is a small rectangular opening at the base of a wall, usually no more than eight inches high, to allow rabbits, hares and other small creatures to pass through on their travels. Larger holes sometimes called 'sheep creeps' are a window like opening in the wall at ground level with a lintel across the top. Sometimes these are also called 'hog holes'. Not only were they built for sheep but also creatures such as badgers and foxes could use them. Badgers are prodigious diggers. Without these holes creatures wanting to get to the other side of a long stretch of gateless wall would otherwise have to burrow beneath it. This weakens the wall itself perhaps to the extent of it ultimately collapsing.

It is estimated at least fifteen species of birds often use walls for nesting, fourteen species of butterflies, ten different species of snails, some twenty species of spiders and harvestmen not to mention six varieties of woodlice, four species of wasps and five of bees. Hornets and earwigs can also be found within. Other creatures that can be found include slowworms, common toads, lizards, house mice, grass snakes and not forgetting the only poisonous snake in the U.K., the adder or viper. Snails are very common wall lovers.

Older dry stone walls are often covered in many genera of plants. Lichens, the earliest forms of plants life, favour exposed faces of walls especially in the pollution free atmospheres of the countryside. Where walls are found in the more damp and shaded areas mosses, algae and liverworts proliferate. These plants provide compost for other plants to thrive such as stonecrop, cranes-bill, Devil's sheep's-bit along with ivy and ferns. In valley walls close to the sea environment valerian is prolific This can be red, white or pink. Foxgloves also colonise walls and can be pink or white.

Plants sometimes escape from gardens either by seeding or people dumping unwanted ones. These, such as aubretia and dianthus, once homeless, find a new home in the nooks and crannies of walls in sunlit areas, whilst in shaded ones saxifrage can be found. In the upper wall areas gypsophila, helianthemum and polygonum plants can be seen. The top of a wall is a favoured place for aster, campanula and geranium.

In the south western parts of Snowdonia walls often combine stone with an earth bank. As such virtually any flower, grass or fern can flourish. It is estimated that eighty four genera of flowers can be found in or on walls, twenty one types of moss, ten species of ferns, twenty one types of grasses, four species of liverworts and eleven species of lichen. Some wildlife prefer walls that are in the process of falling down as they prefer this semi-dereliction. These encourage creatures more so than a tightly built wall because there are more sheltered spaces. Sadly once a wall has lost more than half of its weight habitats are degraded and lose their viability.

Many walls in valley situations have trees and bushes adjacent to them. As such these can, over time, start the collapse of a wall and need control if a wall is to survive. Roots from large trees can be bridged to allow these to expand allowing tree and wall to co-exist. Many walls, however, are now overgrown and their dereliction is held in place by tree roots, grass, mosses, ferns and flowers. When repairing walls new stone is bare so weathering needs to be encouraged. This can be done by adding soil inside the repair or smearing them with manure. If using the existing stone stones should be replaced with any moss or lichen on the outside face.

Summing up it is obvious there is a huge variety of life dependent on walls. The importance of this habitat cannot be stressed too highly. Walls need preserving and not demolished for ugly, much cheaper, wire fencing to be erected in their place.

1. Brittle Bladder Fern; 2. Broad Buckler Fern;
3. Bracken; 4. Wood Sage; 5. Harebells;
6. Polytrichum Commune; 7. Marsh Thistle

*Dry Stone Walls of Eryri*

1. St. John's Wort; 2. Herb Robert; 3. Scaly Moss Fern; 4. Cushion of moss on wall top; 5. Harts-tongue Fern; 6. Maidenhair Spleenwort; 7. Red Valerian; 8. Pink Valerian; 9. Common Polypody fern; 10. Welsh Poppy and Germander Speedwell; 11. Foxgloves growing from wall

*Dry Stone Walls of Eryri*

1. *Fine-leaved Sandwort;*
2. *Blackberry;*
3. *English Stonecrop;*
4. *Navelwort;*
5. *Vetchling;*
6. *Sheepsbit Scabious;*
7. *Catsear;*
8. *Tormentil;*
9. *Bilberry;*
10. *Common Lizards playing chase*

# The Stone Craftsmen of Eryri Today

*Today's carftsmen, often work in pairs (this pair was working on a wall at Talsarnau) – traditional tools but also a small digger comes in handy*

1. & 2. *Preparing work, clearing out and rebuilding at Penrhyddion, Capel Garmon; 3. Steps crafted into a stone wall near a farmhouse at Rhyd Ucha, Bala (reconstructed by Ifan Lloyd Jones)*

1. & 2. Before and after – an old wall in need of repair at Rhyd Ucha, Bala (reconstructed by Ifan Lloyd Jones)

1. & 2. A low stone wall with fence at a farm near Trawsfynydd (reconstructed by Ifan Lloyd Jones)

# Glossary of Commonly Used Terms

**'A' FRAME** – A wooden or metal frame used as a guide when building

**BATTER** – The inward taper of the wall from its base to its top

**BUCK AND DOE** – A design of coping stones that use alternating large and small upright coping stones

**CLONKS** – These are the large stones in a single wall below the coping stones

**COPESTONES** also **COPING STONES** – These are the top most stones to form a decorative effect.
Can also be called **'cams'**, **'tops'** or **'toppers'**

**COURSE** – The horizontal layer of stones placed in the wall

**COVERBAND** – These are large flat stones placed across the width at the top of the wall as a base for the coping stones. Sometimes called **'covers'**

**CRIPPLE HOLE** – The name for a small, low rectangular opening at the base of a wall to allow the passage of sheep. Also has other names such as **hog hole, sheep run, sheep smoose, thawl or thirl hole**. See below for **lunky hole** and **smoot hole**

**DOUBLE, DOUBLING** or **DOUBLE DYKING** – Is a term used for a dry stone wall built with two faces of stones. Between these is the hearting

**DYKING** – The Scottish term for a dry stone wall

**END STONE** – This is the large coping stone placed on top of a wallhead

**FOUNDATION** – The first layer using large stones at the base of the wall. These are sometimes called 'footings'

**GALF STONES** – These are stones that are three quarters the width of the wall. They are placed on alternate courses so that they overlap in the centre of the wall

**GALLOWAY DYKE** – A wall or dyke having the lower third 'doubled' and the upper two thirds single walling

**GAP** – A breach in the dry stone wall. The repair of 'gap' is called 'gapping'. The person who repairs the wall is often called a 'gapper'

**HEARTING** – The small stones used as packing in a double wall

**LUNKY HOLE** – This is a small rectangular hole at the base of the wall to allow a small stream to flow. See above for other terms

**PINS** or **PINNINGS** – Small usually tapered stones used to wedge the building stones securely in place or coping stones

**RETAINING WALL** – A dry stone wall built into the face of a bank to prevent the land behind it slipping down

**ROOD** – a measurement of six yards in granite areas such as Snowdonia. In limestone area it is seven yards. This also equates to how much wall a single 'waller' can build

**SCARCEMENT** – A small ledge of two inches or so at the base of the wall formed by the foundation stones

**SINGLE DYKE** – A wall built with single stones going through the width of the wall

**STILE** – A set of steps over, or a narrow opening through a wall, designed for the passage of people but not livestock. Steps are through stones set in the wall enabling people to climb over. These are known as Stone Step Stiles. Another form of stile is wood ladder erected over both sides of a wall

**STOOP** – This is a large upright monolith set against the wall head

**SMOOT HOLE** – A small rectangular opening designed to allow rabbits, hares and other small creatures to pass. Where hares are the predominant users the term used is '**jook hole**'. See above for other terms

**THROUGHSTONES** – These are the large stones placed at regular intervals across the width of the wall to tie the two sides together

**TRACE WALLING** – The incorrect placing of stones with their length along the face of the wall as opposed to placing them into the wall

**WALLHEAD** – The vertical end of a length of wall, sometimes called a '**cheekend**' or simply '**head**'

**WATERSHOT** – Building stones with their outer faces slightly lower than the centre of the wall

# Useful Contacts

**DRY STONE WALLING ASSOCIATION (D.S.W.A.)**
Lane Farm
Crooklands
Milnthorpe
Cumbria
LA7 7NH
Tel: 015395 67953
Web: www.dswa.org.uk
Email: information@dswa.org.uk

**BRITISH TRUST FOR CONSERVATION VOLUNTEERS (B.T.C.V.)**
The Conservation Volunteers
Gresley House
Ten Pound Walk
Doncaster
DN4 5HX
Tel: 01302 388883
Email: information@tcv.org.uk

**SOUTH COURT ENVIRONMENTAL LTD**
34 Bostock Avenue
Northampton
NN1 4LW
Tel: 01604 630719

Stone Wall Craftsmen in Eryri (as portrayed in this book):

**Stonemasonry Services | Ifan Lloyd Jones**
**Saer Maen - Stone Mason | Wales**
www.ifanlloydjonessaermaen.co.uk

# Further Reading

**BUILDING AND REPAIRING DRY STONE WALLS** by R. Tufnell
ISBN 0-9512306 2 X

**DRY STONE WALLING** by Col. F. Rainsford–Hannay
ISBN 0950262307

**DRY STONE WALLS** by Lawrence Garner
ISBN 0 747806202

**WHAT'S ON A WALL – The Ecology of Walls** produced by South Court Environmental Ltd
ISBN 1 901676 20 X

**DRY STONE WALLING – Techniques and Traditions** published by the Dry Stone Walling Association (D.S.W.A.)
ISBN 0 9512306 8 9

**WALLS IN THE LANDSCAPE** produced by the D.S.W.A.
ISBN 978-0-9568458-2-5

**DRY STONE WALLING** revised by Elizabeth Agate with Sean Adcock
ISBN 0-95467521 9 2

**DRY STONE WALLING** produced by the British Trust for Conservation Volunteers (B.C.T.V.)

**THE HOLE IN THE WALL** An A6 size book especially suited to those under five years old

**DRY STONE WALLS – THE NATIONAL COLLECTION** published by the D.S.W.A.
ISBN 0 9512306 6 2

**IN THERE SOMEWHERE** by David Griffiths and published by the D.S.W.A.
ISBN 0 9512306 5 4

**CONSERVING THE FLORA OF LIMESTONE DRY STONE WALLS** by John Presland. Published by the Wiltshire Natural History Publication Trust

### DVD's OBTAINABLE FROM THE D.S.W.A.

Dry Stone Walling: the essential guide

The Wall Walks the Fell

Dry Stone Country

How to Build & Repair Dry Stone Walls

## COMPACT CYMRU
– MORE TITLES:

www.carreg-gwalch.cymru

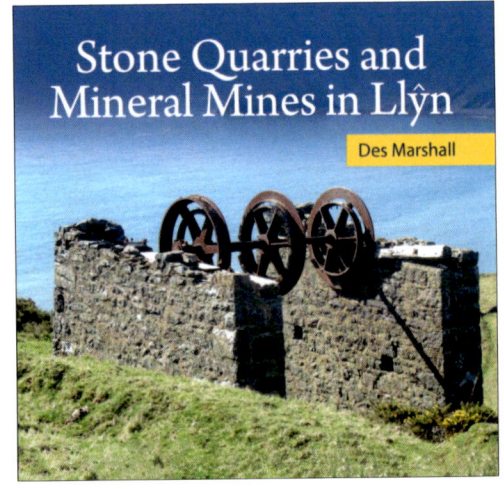

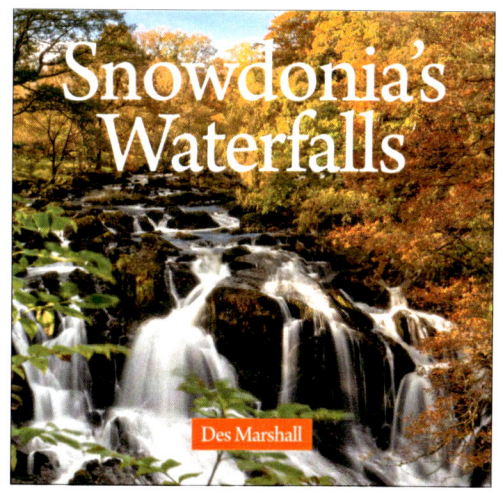
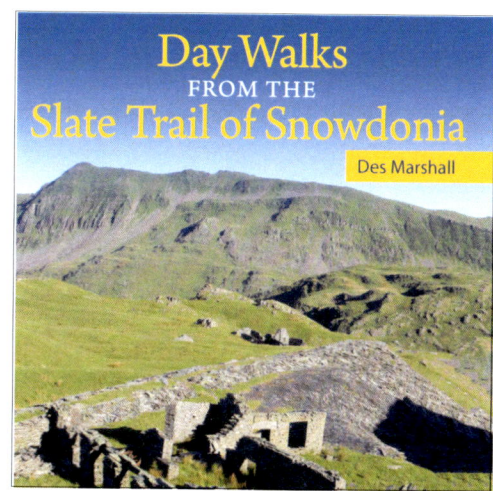

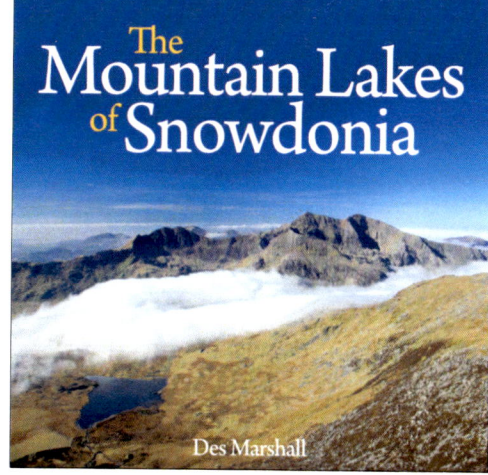

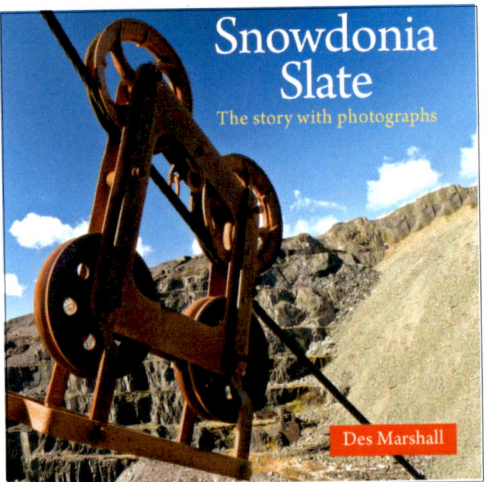

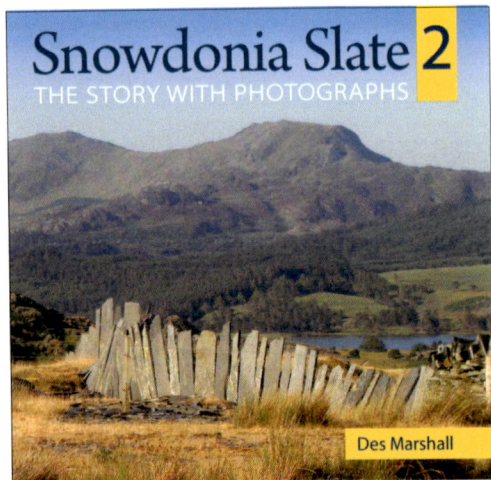

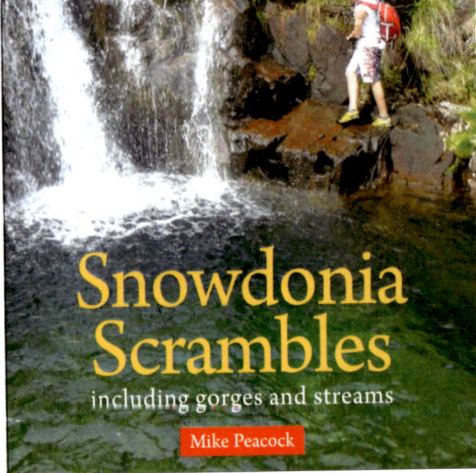